By the cr

Day

1

John 19:25

"But standing by the cross of Jesus were His mother, and His mother's sister, Mary the wife of Clopas, and Mary Magdalene."

You might be wondering why we are meditating this scripture; this scripture does not have much to say but only informs us of those who stood with Christ in His most painful moments by the cross. These were the people that were with Christ in the good times and also in the glorious moments of His ministry.

There were so many that knew Jesus, many came to Him for healing and miracles and some were delivered and set free by his compassion and mercy. But where was all these people when Christ was crucified? the people He fed, the people He taught, the people that followed Him?

Only a few stood with Jesus when he went through crucifixion, because they understood His love and sacrifice. Let us be like these people, lets stand with others in their times of pain, distress, failure and shame when no one else would. Faithful to one another.

"Father we thank you, give us the heart to stand with people in their hardest of times, not just in the fun and happiness. Let we be like these people in the scripture. In Jesus name I pray. Amen"

Word of the cross

1 Corinthians 1:18

"For the word of the cross is foolishness to those who are perishing, but to us who are being saved it is the power of God."

You might be aware of Ash Wednesday the beginning of the lent season, most important period I would say in the Christian calendar. Its importance is the foundation of the Christian faith where man's sins were atoned and washed as Jesus paid the price for it all on the cross.

The message of the cross is foolish for those that fail to understand the power behind it, but for those who have been saved and redeemed, we should understand the power of the cross, especially in a season like this. Sins dominion was demolished, and Christ conquered over darkness.

Let this season not be a passing cloud to you, take this season seriously with mediations of the cross through the word (bible). For those who take the meditation of crucifixion seriously and observe it with reverence, the power of the cross will manifest in your lives.

"Father we thank you for this day, let me not be like a fool and disregard this season and its importance. Fill me with the power of the cross. In Jesus name. Amen"

Boasting

Galatians 6:14

"But may it never be that I would boast, except in the cross of our Lord Jesus Christ"

The word boasting has many definitions but the common thing which strikes out is that it's something that we speak about excessively, meaning that it could be an achievement or an ability which we are proud of. Here in our meditation, we understand the only thing we should be proud about or talking excessively is the Cross of Christ.

What Jesus did on the cross for us is not achievable by any human efforts. For our sins have been washed and we have been reconciled to God , through which we have access to eternal life in heaven. This thing cannot be done through money, or someone's hard work.

Our achievements, our abilities are all temporary and fade and eventually die. What Jesus did on the cross can never fade or die, it's for eternity and cannot be reversed. Do not boast on anything other than what Jesus Did for you on the cross. Talk about it excessively, be proud of what He did for you. *(share the Gospel)*

"Father we thank you , what Jesus did on the cross for us still works in our lives today. Let me not be shy but boast on the cross of Christ. In Jesus name. Amen"

Betrayal

Luke 22:22

"The Son of Man will go as it has been decreed. But woe to that man who betrays him!"

As we are in a season of meditating the cross, we must understand that it all started with betrayal. Jesus was so fruitful in His ministry; His name began to spread throughout the land, and many came to Him for His teachings and to witness the healing miracles.

Out of the 12 one agreed to betray Jesus and Jesus knew about this as He mentions it in the last supper that they have together. Before the cross, before Gethsemane it was Betrayal. Betrayed by the one who He taught, the one He chose and called.

Sometimes people betray us, talk behind us, and do things behind without our knowledge. It's very painful and heart aching when it does happen. We might be carrying such things in our lives, let it be crucified on the cross this season. Your sufferings are no match for what God has planned for you.

Father I thank you; I remember how you were betrayed but you overcame and carried on till resurrection. Let betrayals not kill me but make me stronger. In Jesus name. Amen"

<table>
<tr><td>**Day**

5</td><td># On His body

1 Peter 2:24</td></tr>
</table>

"and He Himself bore our sins in His body on the cross, so that we might die to sin and live to righteousness;"

Who could tell us about the cross better than Peter and here he tells us something exceptionally important that we must all inscribe in our hearts. Jesus bore our sins on His body at the cross, taking all the power and dominion of sin in our lives so that we might not die in sin but die to sin.

When we remember that our sins were on His body and He had to endure the pain and suffering as the outcome of it; it should really make one think about our attitude towards sin. It cannot be alive and active in our lives if its dead. We should access its reign, in and around us.

No one can be sin free and claim to live a life without sin, but one can claim that they are dead to sin; not desiring or indulging in the ways of sin but are seeking righteousness, to act contrary to the sinful nature; through the remembrance of the cross. Do not carry it in your lives.

"Father I thank you for this day, I thank you for bearing my sins on your body so that I might die to it and live-in righteousness. Take away the dominion of sin in my life. In Jesus name. Amen"

Take your cross

Matthew 10: 38

"And he who does not take his cross and follow after Me is not worthy of Me.

What is Jesus trying to tell us here? It seems to be a strong statement from our Lord, and it is with reason; He was aware that each person has a cross that they must carry and also follow Him. It's not about the physical cross Jesus was talking about here.

Every individual on earth has a cross to carry, something heavy, painful, overwhelming beyond their strength. But Christ expects us to carry this cross and follow Him. We all have problems in our lives, some we share some we don't. We cannot give up our faith in the storm or in the struggle, as it is the place where God's grace and strength is revealed.

Sometimes we must endure certain things in our lives but remain steadfast in our prayer and faith, as this will make you stronger and bolder in Christ. Do not listen to the counsel of men or expect them to carry your cross, they will not.

"Father I thank you for this day, I receive grace this day to carry my cross and follow you for I know resurrection awaits after the cross. In Jesus name I pray. Amen"

Bearing the cross

Matthew 10: 38

"As they were coming out, they found a man of Cyrene named Simon, whom they pressed into service to bear His cross.

This is by far one of the most important moments in the crucifixion process, as we see a character who appears for the first time in the gospel for one purpose, to help Jesus bear the cross as Jesus was suffering to a point, He could not carry on further.

How wonderful it would have been for Jesus to have someone help him at this time of pain and agony, someone to ease of the pain from carrying the cross, a helping hand in the most painful moment. This character carried the cross for Jesus.

We are not just called to live our lives eating and drinking and buy homes then die. We are called to serve others through the love of Christ. How many people's crosses do we help to carry; in order to ease their burdens. We should be like this character, a person who was partakes with someone in their toughest of moments.

"Father I thank you for this day, let me be like this character, let me help people with their cross just to ease their pain. In Jesus name I pray. Amen"

Who you are

<table>
<tr><td>Day</td></tr>
<tr><td>8</td></tr>
</table>

Luke 23: 37

"and saying, "If You are the King of the Jews, save Yourself!"

Most of us have watched the cross scenes in various Christian gospel films and pictures. One of the unforgettable scenes prior to crucifixion is when Jesus is questioned. They asked Him a question which is our scripture for meditation. " Are you the king of the Jews"

We all know that Jesus was and is indeed the King of the Jews, King of all Kings but they did not believe. They expected a king to be with riches of the world, army, power, and a big palace. Just because they did not believe who He was does not mean He is not the King of the Jews.

We see Jesus, silent, calm, and quiet whilst under trial, He could have called on angels to come and destroy everyone in that place, He did not boast of His power or try to prove them of who He was. He humbled Himself and let the Father prove who He was. Let God prove you; Let God prove your heart.

"Father I thank you for this day, Lord let me be like you and not boast of myself or try to prove myself, I leave it in your hands. In Jesus name. Amen"

His love for us

Romans 5:8

"But God shows his love for us in that while we were still sinners, Christ died for us."

This is a wonderful passage for us to meditate in this lent season, knowing that God went to an extent of allowing Jesus to die for us so that we would not be thrown to the pits of hell fire. We all know that the scripture says " the wage of sin is death" but God did not want us to die.

The one thing that is so vivid for me as I meditate this scripture is that, while we were still sinners, Christ died for us. We would not give up our lives or the comforts of this life for anyone, especially if that person was a sinner, someone who did not deserve it. But Jesus knowing our sins and faults, still chose to die for us on the cross.

The bible says Jesus Christ is the same yesterday, today, and tomorrow, nothing can separate or change the love He has for us. However, people are not the same, so do not be upset when people's love change, you have His love for eternity.

"Father we thank you for your love, knowing we were sinners, still you chose to die for us so that we wouldn't be punished. We thank you. In Jesus name I pray. Amen"

With a kiss

Mark 14: 45-46

"Going at once to Jesus, Judas said, "Rabbi!" and kissed him. The men seized Jesus and arrested him."

Judas was one among the twelve, someone in the inner circle of Jesus Christ; he had a privilege that many others did not get, he was a chosen disciple called out by the Lord. The sad thing about Judas is that he never knew the value of Jesus.

As we are meditating about the events of the cross, we must examine our circles, especially the ones in the inner circle. Not everyone with us will love us and be sincere to us. But look at the attitude of Jesus, knowing Judas is betraying Him, He still allowed Judas to come and kiss Him.

Judas who had a high calling, chosen and called by the son of God, had an unbelievable sad ending, hung on a tree as he could not bear the guilt of betraying Christ. Christ means the anointed one; it does not end well for anyone who raises against the God's anointed .

"Father we thank you for this wonderful day, help me never speak against the anointed, I pray I have good Godly people in the inner circle. In Jesus name. Amen"

Fixing our eyes

Hebrews 12:2

"fixing our eyes on Jesus, the pioneer and perfecter of faith."

You might be wondering what this scripture has to do with the cross; In this season we should be looking to Christ not only to be washed and cleansed but so that our faith is perfected by Jesus Christ, who is the perfecter of faith.

We learn from the bible that everyone has a different measure of faith, but no one has perfect faith as it has to be perfected through the journey we live on this earth. No one can say I have perfect faith. In this season we should be made strong on the inside, in our faith.

There is only one way that anyone can achieve a good faith filled life, by fixing our eyes on Jesus, His life, His words, His broken body, and His blood which was shed on the cross. Let your eye be fixed only on Christ, do not take your eyes of Him this season.

"Father we thank you for this wonderful day, I bless this day and surrender it to you. Help me with my faith and to fix my eyes on you. In Jesus name. Amen"

The curse

Galatians 3:13

"Christ redeemed us from the curse of the law by becoming a curse for us"

We must meditate daily on one important thing which took place on the cross. As it is written in the scriptures cursed is anyone who is hung on a tree. But Jesus was a sinless person, so pure and holy, why was he hung on a tree?

Our scripture for meditation says "He became a curse for us" it should have been us on the tree, for our sins brought curse on our lives. We carry some through our father our or mother because of generational events, this is also known as the sins of our forefathers.

But we should be grateful, on the cross all our curses were broken, He paid the price for our sins and our curses, not matter what they were. Jesus settled it all on the cross. Know that there is no curse in your lives, as Jesus has dealt with it already.

"Father I thank you for this day, thank you for breaking all the curses away from my life. I refuse to live with it and break it completely In Jesus name. Amen"

Day
—
13

Paradise

Luke 23: 42 - 43

"Then he said, "Jesus, remember me when you come into your kingdom. Jesus answered him, "Truly I tell you, today you will be with me in paradise."

As we are in a season of meditating the events of crucifixion and the cross, this scripture is also something that we should investigate and learn from. There were two robbers that were also sentenced to crucifixion on the cross for the crime that they committed.

One of the robbers hurled insults at Jesus as did the passers-by, mocking Him and teasing Him. But one of the two robbers however looked to Jesus for forgiveness and mercy, and he was pardoned and forgiven; Jesus assured him that he will be with Him in Paradise.

Even in the last stage of this robbers life he was forgiven and not condemned, all this robber did was to humble himself and look to the Lord for His mercy and forgiveness. As a result he was taken to paradise with Christ. People condemned him and punished him to death, but Christ gave him eternal life.

"Father thank you for this day, help me to humble myself and seek your mercy at all times. For your love and compassion are not like the mans. In Jesus name I pray. Amen"

They will know

Mark 15:39

"When the centurion, who was standing right in front of Him, saw the way He breathed His last, he said, "Truly this man was the Son of God!"

When watching the passion of Christ movie, which shows us a detailed account of the events of the cross, we can see a scene when the centurion confesses that Jesus Christ is the Lord and falls to his feet. This was an act of repentance and guilt for what he did to Jesus.

Jesus was mocked, spat at, and stripped naked as well as getting severely beaten up. In all this Jesus never reacted to them or showed them anger but love and pity as they did not understand who He was. But at the cross this centurion saw the light and did accept He was the son of God.

The same centurion would have been the one to crucify Him and would have had heavy involvement in the whole process. But he got to know who Jesus was, the Father proved Jesus, the Father will prove you. People will change their minds about you.

"Father I thank you for this day, forgive my sins against you. I pray that people who have hurt me and broken me will know who I am. Prove me Father. In Jesus name. Amen"

Crown of thorns

John 19: 2

"The soldiers twisted together a crown of thorns and put it on his head. They clothed him in a purple robe"

The crown of thorns that were placed on the head of Jesus Christ is something so vivid that we all remember when it comes to the suffering of our Lord. As I was meditating on this scripture, I came to realise that it was twisted together by the soldiers; specifically tailored to cause excruciating pain.

Sometimes people twist things together and put them on our heads and its specifically done to cause havoc and pain in our heads. The thorn is an object which so sharp that it can penetrate through the flesh and bones, like wise some things people put on our heads can penetrate through to our soul and wound the inner man.

Jesus went through the pain of the thorns so that we would not have to go through these things, people might put things in your head to wound you, break you and cause pain to you. But the Father crowned Jesus as the King of kings. I'm sure the King of kings' crown would be no match for the crown of thorns.

"Father I thank you for this day, whatever is causing pain and havoc in my head I break in Jesus name. every twisted thing devised against me, let it fail in Jesus name. Amen"

Forgive them

Luke 23: 34

Jesus said, "Father, forgive them, for they do not know what they are doing."

As many of you might be aware, today is Mother's Day and I wish all the mothers a blessed Mother's Day. Why is this day celebrated around the world? What is so special about mothers? We can all agree it is because of the Love that a mother gives; and the sacrifices they make for that love. Its special and its unique.

You might be wondering what this has to do with today's devotion, and this season, it is truly relevant indeed, especially in this season of meditation. The bible says " even the mother may forget her infant, but I will never forget nor forsake ". Jesus is the perfect example of a motherly love.

No matter what the child does, the mother's love never changes, her perspective of the child is different to the others, even in the own family. God is not only our Father but our mother as well. No one can love, protect, and defend us like Him.

"Father we thank you for your love, for sending your only son because of your love for us. We pray for all the women and mothers in the world. In Jesus name. Amen"

Exchange of love

Luke 23: 34

" He released the man who had been thrown into prison for insurrection and murder, the one they asked for, and surrendered Jesus to their will."

It is the Roman custom to release a prisoner in the year of jubilee, and Pilate not able to find any faults with Jesus, wanted to release Him. But the Bible clearly describes that the people did not want Jesus to be free, they wanted Barabbas, a murderer. But Jesus kept silent and did not defend nor condemn the release of Barabbas.

Jesus took the place of Barabbas and surrendered to the crucifixion, whilst Barabbas walked free. He exchanged to receive the punishment that was due to Barabbas; I call this the exchange of love. Our lives are remarkably similar to this scenario; what should have fell on us, Jesus took upon Him.

But we were set free on the cross, as Christ was punished for our sins, let us not go back to the same things we were delivered from. We should be grateful in the way we live our lives as a sign of gratitude to the Lord.

"Father we thank you for this day, we remember that you took upon yourself what we deserved as a result for our sins. We thank you Jesus. In Jesus name we pray. Amen"

Prayer prevention

Luke 22: 40

" On reaching the place, he said to them, "Pray that you will not fall into temptation. "

Before everything kicked off in the garden of Gethsemane. Jesus warned His disciples to keep awake and pray so that they will not fall into temptation. The disciples did not understand why Jesus told them to pray, they could not keep awake. But it would have made a massive difference if they did so.

Knowing what was upcoming Jesus instructed them to pray but they did not take heed to His instructions. By prayer we not only diffuse the plan of the enemy but also strengthen our selves in the Lord to withstand the pressure of the storm.

Sometimes it may look as if our prayer is not effective and hence, we might not have the urgency to pray in times of trouble and uncertain forecasts. I encourage you this day to begin to pray, make deposits of prayer over your life.

"Father we thank you for this day, help us to pray and have a strong prayer life Jesus. We ask this in Jesus name. Amen"

Faint spirit

Psalm 142: 3

"When my spirit grows faint within me, it is you who watch over my way. In the path where I walk people have hidden a snare for me."

The psalmist is someone who has faced so many battles not just physically but spiritually and emotionally too from a young age. He also describes how close he was to death at many times. He would go to God and pour his heart out, and each time God would strengthen him.

We must realise that our source of strength, joy and healing only comes from the Lord. When we try to strengthen ourselves through the things of this world, its temporary and can cause more distress. Your source is from heaven.

We must all go to God who is all knowing; only He knows what is exactly going on in your life. Tell God, " I will come to you in prayer everyday Lord without fail", make a declaration of faith. He will make you a strong man, a strong woman.

"Father I thank you for this day, help me when I'm faint, give me the grace to come to you and not go to anyone or anything. In Jesus name. Amen"

Mockery

Matthew 27: 29

" Then they knelt in front of him and mocked him. "Hail, king of the Jews!" they said."

As we are drawing closer to the end of this month, we must keep in mind that we have almost passed many months by the Lords grace. We all get mocked some way or another in life and the intensity of the mockery can vary and can even lead to a breakdown.

One of the Lords suffering was being mocked by soldiers and ungodly people because they could not accept who He was because they had no connection to Him. He was indeed the king of the Jews and the King of Kings.

People will mock us for our dreams (Joseph), our calling (Moses) because they do not understand or accept the plan of God for our lives. Just because people mock us or even our lives look like a mockery, it does not mean God is not able to fulfil His plans for you.

"Thank you, Lord, for this day, help me maintain my peace when things mock me, or people mock me. I trust in your ability and your plans. In Jesus name. Amen"

Into Your hands

<table>
<tr><td>Day
—
21</td></tr>
</table>

Luke 23: 46

"Father, into your hands I commit my spirit! "

Sufferings are an essential part of life; we all must go through some sort of suffering in some way whilst here on earth. It comes in various forms and always uninvited taking us by surprise. Some can be identified by early signs and warnings.

Derek Prince one of my favourite preacher and teacher of the word of God said " there are many forms of storms, some we have to rebuke, some we have to endure, and some are just passing storms. We cannot rebuke all of them and we cannot endure all of them.

Jesus was a very prayerful person, close with the Father and His life was a testimony to what He preached and taught. When facing the crucifixion, rejection and humiliation, He gave Himself and the situation into the Fathers hands. The most secure place on the universe.

"Father I thank you for this day, I commit my life and all that I'm going through into your hands. In Jesus name. Amen"

Hope in Him

Lamentations 3:25

"The Lord is good to those whose hope is in him, to the one who seeks him;"

Hope is a particularly important element in a believers life, I would say it's almost impossible for a believer to live a life for Christ without **hope,** which is grounded in Jesus Christ. We must have it each day, in all circumstances and trials we face.

It is sad to see many in this world have put their hope in stock markets, shares, their employment, money, and savings. All these things can be demolished in a moment, quenching their hopes, and destroying mass amounts of lives.

For us believers who chose to commit and follow the Lord, should not put our hope in the things of this world as it would only bring disappointment and failure. But when we choose to put our hope in Him, we will never fail. Put your hope in Him for everything.

"Father we thank you for this day, we put our hope in you and you alone for everything in our lives. In Jesus name. Amen"

<table>
<tr><td>

Day

___

23
</td><td>

Poured it all

John 19: 34
</td></tr>
</table>

"But one of the soldiers pierced His side with a spear, and immediately blood and water came out."

Commitment is an essential attribute for living an effective and efficient life for the kingdom of God. Who better to meditate in this matter than Jesus Christ our Lord. His commitment knew no bounds, it knew no limits, even to death.

If you are a committed person, you can achieve much more in life. Without commitment to the Lord and His words we can never be successors in Gods kingdom, how far would you go to obey the word of God? How far would you go to be faithful to Jesus? It will cost, sometimes all that you have.

The Father sent Jesus on a mission to save the perishing souls, He was so committed to the calling and to the love of the Father, that He poured out every drop of blood; Giving His life, being broken, bruised, and wounded but that is the price He was willing to pay, and He paid.

"Father we thank you for this day, help me be committed to you and to your word. Let me be ready to pay anything at any cost. In Jesus name."

Sanctify

Hebrews 13:12

" Therefore, Jesus also, that He might sanctify the people through His own blood,"

We all know from the scriptures that there is no remission for sin without the shedding of the blood hence in the old testament animals were sacrificed and their blood was shed to atone for the peoples sins. People made it a custom to sin and bring an animal not fully repenting and turning from their ways.

No animal could cleanse and give a full atonement for the sins of man, as the sins of the world arose to heaven arousing God's anger. God decided to send His one and only Son that He might die and shed His blood to atone for the sins of man once and for all.

In this precious season, pray to God and cleanse yourself from sin and ungodliness. Sanctify your house, your belongings, your body, mind, and soul. His blood has the power to break the dominion of evil, sin and its power from your life.

"Father we thank you for this day, I sanctify my heart, my body and my mind with your precious blood. I make peace with you almighty God. In Jesus name. amen"

Record of debt

Colossians 2:14

"By cancelling the record of debt that stood against us with its legal demands. This he set aside, nailing it to the cross."

What really happened on the cross of calvary thousands of years ago; spiritually for you and me. The scripture for our meditation today is the perfect explanation of the outcome of the blood of Jesus shed on the cross. Everything recorded against us, our sins and our penalties were all cancelled.

Some of us receive fines and penalties for certain things we do wrong such as parking violations, throwing rubbish and speeding. Until we have paid the debt for doing wrong it would keep on accumulating. We would wish that the record would just be cancelled, and we would not have to pay.

Jesus cancelled all your record ; hence you would not pay the price and be thrown to hell but have eternal life; how gracious God is towards us. Let us praise and thank Him and be grateful for what Jesus did.

"Father we thank you for this day, we thank you for cancelling all our records that stood against us. In Jesus name. Amen"

New garments

John 20: 6

" Then Simon Peter came along behind him and went straight into the tomb. He saw the strips of linen lying there,"

As we are in a season of meditation about the cross, we must understand that this season is full of abnormal grace for anyone seeking God for changes, to let go of all old things, natures, habits, and anything that we need to let go of.

The bible verse that we are meditating has an important significance to our cross meditation and is most relevant at this season. When Peter ran to the tomb to see if Jesus had really risen; the tomb was indeed open and looking into the tomb he saw the strips of linen lying there and Peter knew Jesus had risen.

The grave clothes that were wrapped around Jesus were neatly folded and lying in the tomb, the Father exchanged His old dead garments full of blood stains and death odour. He had a new garment, a garment of resurrection, power, and glory. A new garment for you, is waiting.

"Father I thank you for this day, I thank you for the new garments that you have for me, we receive it in Jesus name. Amen"

No Longer I

<table>
<tr><td>Day
——
27</td></tr>
</table>

Galatians 2:20

" I have been crucified with Christ. It is no longer I who live, but Christ who lives in me. "

This is one of my favourite scripture from the bible, being a small verse, it has so much of meaning and depth. This scripture should be inscribed in our hearts and mind so that we live a non-carnal life in this life that is given to us.

The I should not be present and in dominion over our lives. Me, myself, the I is a dangerous thing as it takes the focus away from God and to us. This can only open doors for pride and haughtiness to enter in our hearts. We all know what comes after that, a fall.

As we are in the holy week lets crucify the I to the cross, its passions, desires, and lust. Is Jesus in control of your life or is it you? Who is making the major decisions in your life? Is it Jesus? Do not let the I lead you or guide you, Let Christ live and reign in your life without any interference and disturbance from the I.

"Father we thank you for this day, we crucify this day all the I nature in our lives. Let it be you and you alone. In Jesus name. Amen"

<table>
<tr><td>Day
—
28</td><td></td></tr>
</table>

Blood of His cross

Colossians 1: 20

"and through Him to reconcile all things to Himself, having made peace through the blood of His cross;"

What a beautiful scripture to meditate in this season, are you lacking peace in your life? Suffering from constant warfare in your mind; restless on the inside. I would like to highlight certain words from today's scripture for your attention.

"Through him" – the blood that made peace on the cross belongs to Jesus Christ; He paid the price so that you would have peace, that is the reason why He shed His blood on the cross. In this season let us ask God to manifest His peace in our lives.

Let not the enemy be in control over your mind, deny every entry of evil into your head by engaging the blood of Jesus that made peace for you on the cross. Let there be peace at your work, your marriage, in your children's lives and in your ministry, Peace belongs to you!

"Father I thank you for this day, I engage the blood of Jesus over my mind and heart and all over my life. I cancel every entry of the enemy in Jesus name. Amen"

IN ME

<table>
<tr><td>

Day

29

</td></tr>
</table>

John 16:33

" I have told you these things, so that in me you may have peace. In this world you will have trouble. But take heart! I have overcome the world. "

Join with me today as we give thanks and walk into another day by God's grace. I pray that this day be a peaceful day for you as you seek the Lord and take refuge in Him and His mercies. The scripture for meditation says this" you will have trouble in this world".

But we don't dwell in trouble, we are not forsaken and left alone to deal with the trouble; we have Jesus who overcame the trouble and tyranny of this world. But we must note that the scripture says there is peace available in Him.

I recall to the scripture which says, " if you remain in me and I in you then you will bear much fruit". We must be one with Jesus, we must align our lives with the co-ordination of the Holy – Spirit. You will overcome trouble and not be overcome by it.

"Father we thank you for this day, we surrender our life into your hands. We give all troublesome circumstance in our life to you. We speak your peace. In Jesus name. Amen"

Remember

Luke 24:7

" He is not here; he has risen! Remember how he told
you, while he was still with you in Galilee:"

Remember resurrection Sunday (Easter Sunday), what a
wonderful day; we should rejoice and celebrate this day every
day as much as the other important days in the Christian
calendar. The resurrection marks the day death was defeated,
and man was redeemed, reconciled back to their creator.

Thousands of years ago, the people that loved Jesus and gave
up everything to follow him, were all scared and filled with
pain and tears, for they were uncertain of what would happen.
Are you in a similar situation? the angel said, " remember how
he told you" (remember the promise).

Yes, it's true we have to carry the cross, we have to endure the
crucifixion of the flesh which is not a pleasant experience and
can be painful for us. But we must remember the things God
has spoken to us, the promises delivered to us in prayer and
through prophecies. Your resurrection is at hand.

"Father we thank you for this day, we remember all that you have
spoken to us. I thank you for my resurrection. In Jesus name. Amen"

<table>
<tr><td>**Day**
―――
31</td><td></td></tr>
</table>

The one

John 11: 25

" The one who believes in me will live, even though they die; "

As the seasons change from winter to summer it shows outwards signs in the temperature and in nature, producing blossoms and buds as a sign to the coming summer. A time when all comes to life and the waiting is over. In winter here in the UK, everything comes to a standstill and dies down due to the harsh cold climate. But everything that died comes back to life better and stronger for summer.

We too might have gone through seasons of standstill and extreme conditions because of winter, but if we are the one who chooses to believe, the one who is waiting patiently, the one whose hope is firmly set one the Lord; our waiting is not wasted and our eyes will see the beautiful new season of flourishment.

The scripture for meditations says, " the one who believes in me", be the one who believes and not doubts, be the **One** and not part of the many who choose not to believe but fall a victim to the harsh seasons.

"Father we thank you for this day, we thank you for giving us grace to believe you and you alone. We do not want to be a part of the many but be the one. In Jesus name. Amen"